THE Last Time I'LL Write About You

DAWN LANUZA

THE LAST TIME I'LL WRITE ABOUT YOU

Copyright © 2016 Dawn Lanuza.

Indie Sisiw Books
Manila, Philippines

www.dawnlanuza.com

Edited by Layla Tanjutco
Illustrations by Luntian Dumlao
Cover art design by Reginald Lapid

THE LAST TIME I'LL WRITE ABOUT YOU

To young hearts,
Keep beating,
Keep breaking,
Keep falling in love.

THE FIRST.

SUNBEAM

You light up the room
Wherever you go
With your wit and charm
You turn things around

You light up the room
You're a rush of blood
You're a ray of sun
You lighten me up.

THE OBJECT OF MY

I love the way you look
Your eyes, they twinkle
Your lips, they curl
Your whole spirit lifts

I love the way you look
As I watch you across the room
That is until you looked at me
And nothing else could compare

WHAT I LIKE ABOUT YOU

Your hand

    How you held the small of my back

Your fingers

    How it grasped mine as we crossed the street

Your feet

    How it led us to your room

The chain on your neck

    How it slid through my fingers as I pulled you
    in

Your eyes

    How it spoke to me

Your bed

    How it welcomed us both

Your lips

    Oh, how it silenced my doubts.

You are the dream

But I've had wake up calls

IN A NUTSHELL

I'm not brave enough to love you

The same way

You're not strong enough to take me on.

"He was good for you.

"Then why'd you let him go?"

"I don't doubt it."

"I wasn't good for him."

BOTTOMLINE

This is how it's going to be:

A million unanswered questions,

A thousand books you'd never ask me to read,

A hundred movies we'd never fall asleep in together,

A couple of songs I won't hear you sing in the shower,

A few words I would never interrupt with a kiss,

A piece of you, I'll miss every single day.

This is how it's going to be.

I should be alright with that.

TRUTH

You read these things
And you ask the world,
Why doesn't it happen
To someone like you?

Deep in your heart,
You knew the answer:
It's because you don't let it.

AND NOW I'M RUINED

When I met you
I've always wondered
How I've never met
Anyone quite like you

When we parted
I've always wondered
How everyone else
Reminded me of you

DECOY

You're not it

Although you filled in that spot quite convincingly

You're not it

Can you get up from that seat so we can move along accordingly?

THE PULL.

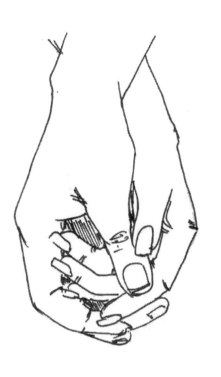

CONFESSION

I told everyone
I love you
Sorry if they knew before you

To be fair,
I think everyone knew
Before I did, too.

CONSISTENCY

I don't think you think of me
The way I think of you
For you do so only sporadically
While I have you in me
Constantly.

HEAD COUNT

How many of us
Have slept in your bed
Which one did you intend to keep

How many of us
Held up your head
While you continued to sleep

How many of us
Believed the promises you made
How many did you let weep

REASONS FOR REJECTION

I hope you know
I said no
Not because I didn't want to

I knew better than to rush it
We always seem to fall
Into each other too easy

So much so that when we part
It's like velcro
Gone, in a blink of an eye

Painless then
But the sound lingers
Then haunts

I hope you know

I want more

Than that day stretched into hours

I want you every day

Kissing me good night

Til tomorrow

And tomorrow

And tomorrow

And tomorrow

And tomorrow

And tomorrow.

HH

You're the face of innocence
Of sunny days,
Long and leisurely walks
And happy talks

I liked remembering you this way.

You're the face of change
Of late nights,
Beer bottles, ashtrays
And ignored calls.

You broke my heart this way.

You're the face of my youth,
Of second and too many chances,
Two clasped hands
At the back of the car.

I wish we could have just stayed.

THE NTH BREAKFAST

Hot coffee
Burnt tongue
Confiding exclusively
Of woes unsung

Warm hands
Kind smile
Eyes seeking to understand –
But you lie.

METAMORPHOSIS

for Anton

I built a cocoon made of stories of you.
I intend to stay with your memories
Where it's warm and good.

I built a cocoon made of stories of you.
But one day,
I'll have to break through.

THE KISS.

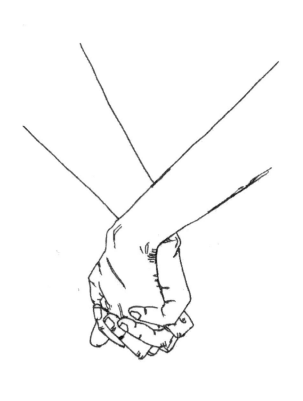

RATIONALE

All this time you've been trying
To undress me
From head to toe

All this time I've insisted
That I got scars
Underneath it all

All this time that you don't have anymore
All these fears that I've kept close

Yet

All this time, I've been unraveling
With all these hopes that you're still watching

I doubt it.

But here you go.

6 A.M.

Waking up is never the same
Not without your arms tangled up in mine
Not without your kiss on my cheek
Not without you telling me,
"You look beautiful today."

OTHER MEANS OF COMMUNICATION

I like how our hands seem to have their own conversations, apart from our mouths

I like how we tell things we can't seem to say out loud

In these spaces between,

Our fingers meet,

And they fit.

Perfectly.

There were no walls.

No secrets.

I like how our hands knew how to be together

At times we can't seem to.

RESOLVE

I could keep saying

One more

Just one more

But when does it end?

REFLECTION

The thing is,
I used to remember your laugh.
I hear it behind my ear,
It tickles me.

I feel your breath.
I sense your nerves.
I keep this memory of you
For the longest time.

Now that I've forgotten
I tried to remember
Trust me,
I'm the only one left trying to remember

What it's like to have you near
That I can feel your breath
The tremble in your voice
As it creates waves in me

Stirring,
Kneading,
Making me faint.

This is all imaginary
For I can no longer remember.
I am only creating the memory.

This is no longer you.
This is all me.

NORTHERN STAR

Look up the sky
Like once upon a time
Look up and I
Will guide you back to me.

I meant to keep you

But I didn't want to be kept

See the problem?

MODERN VAMPIRES

The sun burns my skin
In your bed as we lay
It's a clear sign:
We're not made for the day.

We're creatures of the night
Straddled in the sheets
The dawn is in sight
We part as soon as we meet.

THE TALK.

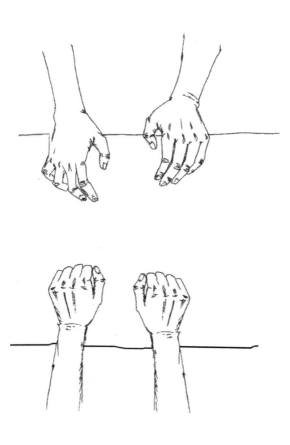

SUSTENANCE

When I think about you in huge doses,
I drown.
In despair,
In longing,
In guilt.

I learned to think of you
In tiny rations
Like meals delivered to my plate
Three times a day

Each time enough

To nourish me,

To make me hope,

To keep my heart alive.

To keep my heart alive.

THE WORST SLEEPOVER

Is there anything stranger
As sleeping on the same bed
With a man who has changed?

Not in who he was,
But in the way that
He has looked at you.

A week ago he promised
This time, he'll stay
But his eyes are worlds away

You held on to him
In that forsaken bed
He's distant, cold —

Nothing else could be said.

ARE YOU OKAY?

I'm shouting this to the universe

In case you needed to answer.

THE FEAR

I used to thank you
For making me feel beautiful
And you assured me,
I am.

Since you left
All I've felt is horrible
And I'm so scared you realized,
I am.

OUR SONG

That one morning
You told me,
"To the ends of the Earth."
Nothing more.

You were quoting that song
So I didn't say anything
But I keep going back to that
Now that we are on polar opposites.

Intentionally or not
We've drifted apart
But I keep holding on to that
Like a promise

Cause I still think of you
While I'm safely tucked here
Hoping I could reach out
To where you've ran away.

UNASKED QUESTION 1

Was I a secret not worth sharing
Or
Was I a fact not worth telling?

REVOLVING DOOR

Maybe you wanted me to hate you
Cause God knows I love you
Maybe you hate me too
Cause why else would you
Walk in and out of my life
Like you were in a revolving door?

I watch you at it
Spinning and spinning
I wait for you to decide,
To stop,
Look at me,
Come inside.

Stay?

Maybe you wanted me to hate you

Forget that I love you

So I can stop watching

And you can stop spinning

Cause God knows it's exhausting

To be inside that revolving door.

And maybe

Just maybe

That's why you hate me

Cause it was just you spinning

As it always has been

In that revolving door.

THE HURT.

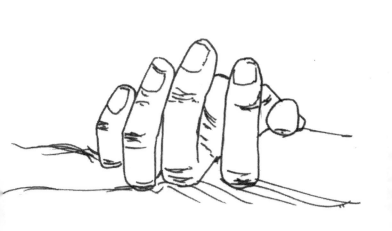

MEMENTO

Throughout the years we've kept:

Tickets to concerts

Stubs from movies

Prize toys from cereal boxes

Notes scribbled

Books swapped

CDs burned

I don't know what we were thinking.

Now that we're apart

I have all of your stuff.

I asked you, should I return it?

You said, hold on to it.

Then added,

It's a reason for us to see each other again.

The last time we talked
We mentioned these mementos ∕
Things that were not ours but in our possession.

I lost your book, you said.
I have your favorite movie, I claimed.
Keep it, you concluded.

Somehow keeping it
Wasn't as comforting
As holding on to it
So we can see each other again.

When did we become such a bad idea?

THE MENTOR

Teach me how to forget
Like how you taught me your name
These words, what they meant
And which one you liked best.

Teach me how to forget
Like how you taught me to say
Good morning, good night,
Every damn day of our lives.

Teach me how to forget
Like how you taught me your secrets
Silly jokes, careful confessions
Anecdotes and one liners

Teach me how to forget

Like how you taught me to believe

How easy it was to disappear

Over

And

Over

Until I can no longer remember

The last time you were there.

IN HINDSIGHT

Darkness is a friend
We've been long acquainted
It was nice knowing your light
But I couldn't be mended

Sadness is a cloak
I wear around my shoulders
You let the sun soak
On my skin to recover

But the dark, it remains
And you were slowly fading
You bring the sun,
But it keeps on setting.

THE PENSIEVE

I would like to see me in your memory

Maybe then I'd understand

How we turned out to be

From the very best

To this colossal mess

PLEA

You can't help
Those who don't want to be helped
That's what you said,
I heard it.

I can't help
How I felt
This is how I bled
You didn't see it.

I liked you so much that I even dated your friends.

MEMORY

Did you ever talk about me
The way I talked about you?
With a smile or a sigh
Never a frown or a curse

Did I leave you enough memories?
I bleed of your impressions
Your every laugh and musing,
Your stories and dreams.

ROOT

It's funny how
The thought of you makes me mad
When all along I thought
You're the one person I'd exclude from that

That was the problem:
I rooted for you.
And you?
You were just being you.

I expected you to spare me
Of any hurt,
Of any lie
Thinking I deserved it.

Sometimes

I think this hate

Is not because you hurt me

Or because you lied

You proved me wrong

And that stings more

Than all of the things

You've done combined.

THE LAST.

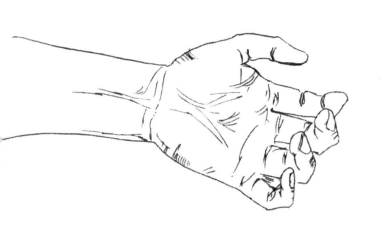

Should I be thankful or regretful

That my only idea of love is you?

FOREIGN BEDS

Late night
In strange places
And foreign beds
I find myself thinking of you
Where you are
How you've been
Who you're with that very second

I don't ask,
For these are simple questions
Only asked by people who matter
Your family,
Your friends,
Your lover.

No longer

Never will be

Me.

BOTH FEET ON SHORE

You're not coming back, are you?
I got used to having you drop by
Every once in a while
That I've convinced myself
That you were coming home

As if you belong with me,
Not out on sea.

ECHOES

Your words
Stuck to my skin
Painted all over
Tattooed well under

Your words
Scarce over the years
Stuck to my head
Played back like a record

I wish I could tell you
All I didn't say then
I wish I could give you
Answers you were searching
I wish you were here,
I wish you were still near.

Your words

Faint as a whisper

Stick to me, still

Cause it's all I have left

Of what we have and what could have been.

STILL

My favorite part of waking up at night
Is realizing that you're holding me
That somehow, our subconscious
Found a way to keep us linked:

Arms around my waist
Thighs interlaced
Foreheads leaning in
Our breaths colliding

It's so quiet,
So calm,
So tranquil,
That I drift off with a grin.

I wake up at night sometimes
Still
Sometimes from a bad dream
Sometimes for no reason at all

Then I feel sorry
For you're no longer there
To wrap me in your arms
And kiss the nightmares away.

THE WORLD IS OUR SOUVENIR

The world remembers
What we try to forget
It's in the embers
Of the things we left

It's in the concrete,
The streets we used to tread
In the halls we used to meet
When we had hours to spend

It's in the book you carried home
In this umbrella we shared
It's in the stars you wished on
In your skin, your palms,
Your fingers: playing with my hair

It's in your unmade bed

The wrinkle, the weight

It's in the distance to the door I travelled

In the silence, partings unsaid.

LESSON

I'm tired of missing you

So I made a point to forget you

But it gets exhausting

Once you learn:

Forgetting is just another form of remembering.

CROOKED

I always felt like
Begging for your forgiveness
For the things I was afraid of
For the things you couldn't fix

But I realized
I never owed you anything
I never needed your approval
I just needed to forgive myself

I found myself, bent:
Never quite broken,
Never quite lost,
Never quite yours.

I just want to stop wasting the time
I've been wasting on you.

EPILOGUE

Despite everything
I still thank the universe
For blessing me with you
As my first

If I could love you this much
For this long
— And on my first try —
Then surely,

I could love someone else more
Far better,
Far longer.

P.S.

Think of it as cruel
Think of it as hateful
None of this is true
Believe it or not at all

This started out for you
Only it ended for me
So with finality:
This is the last time I'll ever write about you.

ABOUT THE AUTHOR

Dawn Lanuza writes contemporary romance and young adult novellas. This is her first poetry collection. She works for the music industry by day and writes meet cutes and snappy comebacks by night.

Her first book The Boyfriend Backtrack, published by Anvil Publishing, was nominated for the Filipino Readers' Choice awards for Romance in English in 2015.

She currently lives with a very spoiled cream toy poodle.

Contact her at:
  www.dawnlanuza.com
  dawn.lanuza@gmail.com
  www.facebook.com/AuthorDawnLanuza
  Twitter: @dawnlanuza

ALSO BY DAWN LANUZA:
  The Boyfriend Backtrack
  What About Today
  The Hometown Hazard